Give Me a Break

Give Me a Break

For Women Who Have Too Much to Do

by Leigh Anne Jasheway
Edited by Cindy Cashman

Andrews and McMeel
A Universal Press Syndicate Company
Kansas City

ISBN: 0-8362-2151-6

Library of Congress Catalog Card Number: 96-83991

ATTENTION: SCHOOLS AND BUSINESSES

Andrews and McMeel books are available at quantity discounts with bulk purchase for educational, business, or sales promotional use. For information, please write to: Special Sales Department, Andrews and McMeel, 4520 Main Street, Kansas City, Missouri 64111.

You know you're under too much stress if:

Your inner child wants to be adopted.

....

Your favorite flavor of ice cream is cherry vanilla Maalox.

....

You have a nervous twitch that registers on the Richter scale.

....

You have that Prozac look.

....

The last time you had your blood pressure measured,
the cuff exploded.

....

It's been so long since you've had your
hair done that the neighbor kids
refer to you as The Troll.

....

Your muscles are so tense, the local massage therapy school uses you as a teaching model.

....

Your favorite pizza topping is Rolaids.

....

Your favorite color is Pepto-Bismol.

....

You fall asleep counting things on your "To Do" list.

....

You call people on the phone and then
forget who you are.

....

You bite someone else's fingernails off.

....

You consider Susan Powter laid back.

....

Your stress management coach told you to visualize
something that makes you feel peaceful inside.
You visualize strangling your boss.

....

You've tried using worry beads,
but you keep crushing them.

....

You started your own support group, but the other
members ask you to leave.

....

You can only relax to music played backward.

....

You bought a pyramid to sit under for relaxation,
but it gets in the way when you pace.

....

You tried going to an acupuncturist for stress management, but you couldn't sit still, and you lost a gallon of blood.

....

Your idea of a balanced meal is a Bloody Mary and a multivitamin.

....

Your neck and shoulders are so full of knots, local Boy Scouts get badges for visiting you.

....

Your glad clothes from the '70s are back
in style again — that's the last chance you had
time to go shopping.

....

You know it's going to be a stressful day when:

The string pulls out of your tampon.

....

You can't get the top off the Midol bottle.

....

You have to sue your support hose for support.

....

You've had your eight glasses of water with lunch and there's a sign on the door of the Ladies' Room that says "Out of Order."

....

You have bad hair AND a yeast infection.

....

You have an appointment with your gynecologist and a tax audit.

....

Your tummy-control panties explode during lunch.

....

You run into that cute guy you've been wanting to talk to at the grocery checkout while buying super absorbent maxi-pads.

....

Your zipper only goes halfway up and it's not even that time of the month.

....

You're on a long car trip and a sign says, NEXT REST STOP 243 MILES.

....

Sports Illustrated swimsuit edition is on the newsstands again.

....

Your Glamour Shots picture turns out so bad they make you sign a waiver releasing them from all responsibility.

....

Both your flight and your period are late.

....

It's not like you haven't tried to manage your stress

Yoga class was a disaster. The paramedics had to use the jaws of life to get you out of the lotus position.

....

The people at Crisis Hotline call you.

....

You fast-forward your relaxation tape.

....

You were kicked out of the local stress management
seminar for being a bad influence
on the rest of the class.

....

While you listen to a relaxation tape, you do your taxes,
your nails, and your laundry.

....

When your husband found you lying on the floor trying to
meditate, he called the paramedics.

....

You meditate faster than anyone else in your class.

....

When you tried "deep breathing," you inhaled the cat.

....

You bought *Reflections for Women Who Do Too Much,*
but you haven't read it because
you have too much to do.

....

You enjoy the thrill of saving time by doing Yoga while driving.

....

You tried acupuncture — but it makes you want to sing karaoke.

....

Books every stressed-out woman should own (but never have time to read)

Women Who Run with the Wolves,
Run from the Wolves, and
Clean Up after the Wolves.

....

The Seven Habits of Highly Stressful Women.

....

Meditations for Women Who Stress Too Much.

....

Men are from Mars,
Women Have to Clean It Up.

....

Start the Insanity.

....

I'm Okay, You're Annoying Me.

....

The Bridges of Madison County
Have All Washed Out.

....

What Color Is My Blood Pressure?

....

Holiday survival skills for women who stress too much

Only buy gifts for people you actually like.

....

Date a massage therapist.

....

Don't call your depressing friends
until after the holidays.

....

Up your Prozac prescription.

....

Visualize your in-laws far, far away.

....

Instead of comparing your family to the Cleavers
or the Waltons, compare your family to a
really dysfunctional family, like Britain's royal family —
there, now don't you feel better already?

....

Serve pizza or tacos for the big holiday meal.

....

If you absolutely have to volunteer to
be in the church play, don't audition for Mary,
she never had any fun.

....

Put off the chores — tell people the dust is really
expensive imitation snow.

....

Sit in Santa's lap — why shouldn't you get
what you want for the holidays?

....

Give yourself a gift — a vacation, a
full-body massage, . . . whatever works.

....

Move and don't leave a forwarding address — the
relatives will have to visit someone else.

....

Take pictures at the office holiday party that you
can use to get that big raise next year.

....

You know the holiday is going to be stressful when:

Your New Year's resolution is to date a guy who doesn't look better in a dress than you do.

....

Your ex-husband's standing under the mistletoe wearing a shirt that says "This isn't a potbelly, it's the engine of a sex machine."

....

You have to send a Mother's Day card to each of
your mom's seventeen personalities.

....

You have to work overtime on Labor Day.

....

The only thing you can think to be thankful
about at Thanksgiving is that your eyebrows
are finally starting to grow back.

....

At least no one expects you to cook holiday meals — last
year you burnt cornflakes.

....

You're under so much stress, you've developed thousands of bad habits.

You chew used coffee grounds for an afternoon pick-me-up.

....

You wear boxing gloves to keep yourself from gnawing your fingernails down to the bone.

....

You have so little time for exercise that they've named a line of sofas after you.

....

Your idea of regular exercise is running between meetings.

....

You pace so much you've worn a hole in the carpet so deep that you can see the people below.

....

Your nervous foot twitching
wakes you up at night.

....

It's been so long since you laughed that your
funny bone has a stress fracture.

....

You're so agitated at the end of the day, you could
wash a load of clothes in your sleep.

....

You have teethmarks in your steering wheel.

....

You drink so much coffee they've named
a plantation in your honor.

....

You drink so much coffee, Folger's sends
you annual reports.

....

You can't even remember
what it's like to relax.

The last vacation you took was a walk around your office
building — on the ledge, fourteen stories up.

....

If you were stranded on a desert island,
you'd take your unpaid bills, your unread mail,
and a bottle of Tagamet.

....

You and your husband won a second honeymoon
trip for two, but you had to work so
he took the woman next door.

....

The last time you took a break
it was called Recess.

....

The last time you said "No," your mom made
you eat broccoli anyway.

....

The last time you went on vacation,
you wore bellbottoms.

....

The last time you went to church,
Madonna was the statue holding a baby.

....

The last time you went to the dentist,
the tooth fairy visited that night.

....

You're so busy:

You use Lee Press-On Clothes.

....

You think 911 has too many numbers.

....

Your turn signal has been on since 1972.

....

You don't drink cappuccino because
it takes too long to order.

....

You eat your Lean Cuisine frozen.

....

You only watch five of David Letterman's Top Ten list.

....

You go to work with your pantyhose only
halfway pulled up.

....

You're seriously contemplating buying
Depends so you don't have to take time out
to go to the bathroom.

....

You're so busy, your family hardly knows you:

If you were kidnapped, no one would notice.
If the kidnappers put you on the phone to
beg for the ransom money, your family
wouldn't recognize your voice.

....

When you get into bed, your husband pulls a gun
and asks, "What do you want?"

....

Your children call you "Aunt Mom."

....

Your children earn extra money leasing your spot
at the dinner table to strangers.

....

Family life is stressful when:

Your son takes your WonderBra in for Show and Tell.

....

Your three-year-old explains to the nice policeman what color the light actually was when you went through it.

....

You come home to find your husband cleaning the kitchen countertop, which is very nice of him except for the fact that he's using your contraceptive sponge.

....

Your son has to play tartar in the school dental play
and he needs a costume tomorrow.

....

Your husband's favorite basketball team
lost in the NBA finals.

....

You and your husband stay up all night fighting about
whose mother is more annoying.

....

People at work love you because you do all their work for them:

You suffer a slight shock when the cellular phone in your shower shorts out.

....

You have to put "use the bathroom" on your To Do list . . . at the bottom.

....

The evening cleaning lady calls you
"Hey, move your feet."

········

You have more changes of clothes in your file
cabinet than in your closet at home.

········

You accidentally staple the Frederick's of Hollywood
catalog to the back of your big report
and put it on your boss's desk.

········

The last time you came home before dark, the next-door neighbor filed a suspicious person report on you.

....

Your boss gave you luggage for your birthday and one-way tickets to Aruba.

....

Your idea of a good day at work is two days.

....

Your promotion went to the boss's nineteen-year old niece, Tiffany.

....

You listened to a tape of your last
presentation and you sounded
like Bobcat Goldthwait.

....

The last time you took a day off was by mistake
during a total eclipse.

....

Your favorite restaurant is decorated with telephones,
rolodexes, and file cabinets.

....

You juggle so many roles, they've offered you
a part in the circus. And you said Yes
(you don't know how to say No).

....

You are the poster child for Workaholics Anonymous.

....

You don't have an ulcer, you have a black hole.

....

You've worn all the letters off
your computer keyboard.

....

You have so much trouble communicating with your staff that they bought you "English as a Second Language" tapes for your birthday.

....

Your idea of job satisfaction is getting a parking place.

....

Your office chair has a life-support system built into it.

....

Your new boss turns out to be that little nerd you used to call StickBoy in junior high.

....

Your secretary hides from you.

....

You press so hard when you sign your name,
your desk looks like one in a junior high school.

....

You don't have a coffee mug, you have a coffee pitcher.

....

Everyone at the office fights so much, you have been
invited to appear on "Geraldo Rivera." The topic is,
"Coworkers Who Think About Murder."

....

Stress and sex

You've had a headache so long
that the American Medical Association
is using you as a case study.

....

All your lingerie has cutouts — from where the
moths have eaten through.

....

You can't decide if your love life is
more like "America's Funniest Home Videos"
or "Tales from the Crypt."

....

You consider David Letterman's Top Ten lists foreplay.

....

During sex, you fantasize about finishing
that big project at work. You yell out
feverishly, "Fax it now, fax it now!"

....

You fantasize about Mr. Rogers — he has
such a calming voice.

....

You're retaining water and he wants you to wear that
tiny black teddy and make love with the lights on.

....

You only have time for sex during leap years.

....

Your vibrator shorts out and causes a citywide blackout.

....

The last time you slept with someone of the
opposite sex was on a blanket on the floor,
and afterward you had milk and cookies
and sang "Eensy Weensy Spider."

....

You accidentally drop your birth control pill on
the floor and your boyfriend's cat eats it.

....

You think watching *Casablanca* once a year is regular sex.

....

Don't be stressed by sex — use one of these excuses:

Not tonight dear, I have...

A temporary case of sanity

....

A better offer

....

A date

....

A gallon of Ben and Jerry's waiting for me at home.

Stress and the single girl

In order to meet new friends, you submitted
an ad to the classified section
of the local paper. They carried it in
the "Impersonal Column."

....

Your blind date shows up wearing a T-shirt
that says "Rush is Right."

....

The only date you've had all year
was to a benefit dinner for
Women Who Have No Lives.

....

You dated a CPA and when you broke up,
he billed you for his services.

....

You dated a teacher until one night
he only gave you a C–.

....

He excuses himself before ordering his salad — then calls his mom to find out if he likes ranch or bleu cheese.

....

Your date picks you up in a hearse.

....

You told your boyfriend you could cook and now he actually expects you to.

....

Your date brings his parole officer — and she's better looking than you.

....

Last night's date is on tonight's episode of "America's Most Wanted."

········

Your date shows up with tickets to the monster truck rally and matching overalls for the two of you.

········

Your candlelit dinner sets his toupee on fire.

········

Your date has a tattoo that says "Giddy-Up."

········

Your cable goes out and all there is to do is watch his videotape of the NFL.

. . . .

All your friends are pregnant.

. . . .

Your date's curfew is 10:00 P.M.

. . . .

The stress of being home alone:

You subscribe to the new TV service, "Closed-Captioned for the Emotionally Impaired."

....

There are leftovers in your refrigerator that have a more active social life than you do.

....

"E.R." has been preempted for basketball play-offs.

....

"Saturday Night Live" still stinks.

....

You got some houseplants to keep you company, and they all died when you talked to them.

....

You put on your WonderBra to chat on the Internet and no one flirts with you.

....

Your answering machine cuts off in the middle of the phone number of that cute guy you met on the subway.

....

You accidentally wash your favorite lipstick
with a load of whites.

....

You offer to baby-sit your friend's kids only to find out
an hour later that they have chicken pox,
which you have never had.

....

The cockroaches in your kitchen have a
better social life than you do.

....

You're so broke, you fill your blue water
bottles with tap water.

....

The only person who leaves messages on your answering
machine is the MCI representative.

....

It's been so long since you've been on a date,
you could braid the hair on your legs.

....

Dating a younger man can be stressful when:

They card your date, but not you.

....

He finds your collection of anti-aging creams
in the medicine chest.

....

The deepest discussion you've had to date is whether
he is more like Beavis or Butt-head.

....

During sex, you're reminded of the fact that you once baby-sat for kids who are now older than he is.

....

Your dentures get stuck to his retainer.

....

When he takes you out for a dinner show, he takes you to Chuck E. Cheese's Pizza Parlor.

....

His idea of romantic music is MegaDeath.

....

When you hang out with his friends,
all they do is play Nintendo.

....

What you thought was a rush of lust
turns out to be hot flashes.

....

You put on your sexiest nightgown and he says
his mom has one just like it.

....

Who has time for a hobby?

You took up painting to relax and all your pictures look like they were done by Picasso on a really bad day.

....

You took up gardening to relax and your flower bed has a headstone with your boss's name on it.

....

You tried to play the violin to relax, but you sawed right through the strings.

....

Your most relaxing hobby is chainsaw
"Cut by Number" art.

....

You are so competitive, when you run marathons, you
come in first, second, and third in the same race.

....

You play fast polka music to get your
plants to grow faster.

....

You are learning to make explosives at home.

....

Your most relaxing hobby is planning hostile takeovers.

....

You took up oil painting, but you use a
broom to get it done faster.

....

You enjoy logrolling near waterfalls.

....

You know it's going to be a stressful pregnancy when:

The pregnancy indicator stick turns Neapolitan.

....

You accidentally fax your basal temperature chart to the mechanic instead of your gynecologist.

....

Your name is Rosemary.

....

Your ear lobes have actually swelled up.

....

Your inner child has morning sickness.

....

You have to buy your maternity clothes at Tents R Us.

....

You have varicose veins on your forehead.

....

You've called the Psychic Pregnancy Hotline.

....

You just joined the convent.

·· ·· ·· ··

You've just been elected president of
Zero Population Growth.

·· ·· ·· ··

You're not sure you're the real mother.

·· ·· ·· ··

You know it's going to be a stressful menopause when:

Your husband accidentally applies
your estrogen patch instead
of his nicotine patch.

....

You discover that your calcium supplements
expired twenty years ago.

....

You sweat so much your shoes
squish when you walk.

....

Your hot flashes are so strong, you can't
drive a car because the gas tank
might catch on fire.

....

Your mood swings are so severe
that you wear a bumper sticker that says,
"Caution — Wide Turns."

....

You get less sleep than the cast of "E.R."

....

You've heard that some women grow a mustache —
you're growing sideburns.

....

Getting older can be stressful, too. Especially when...

The grocery sacker calls you ma'am.

....

Alpha hydroxy doesn't cut it — you need to sandblast and spackle.

....

You accidentally put creme rinse
in your coffee.

....

Your memory's getting so bad, you keep
forgetting to nag your husband.

....

You notice that when the light
hits you just right, you look
just like your dad.

....

The only thing sagging worse than your hose are your breasts.

....

Your vision is getting so bad, your husband is starting to look good again.

....

Who says exercise reduces stress? How about when...

You go rollerblading and you fall down on the only part of you that wasn't covered by a pad.

....

Your thong leotard gets stuck on the StairMaster.

....

Your favorite exercise video is Roseanne's *Bitch Fitness*.

....

You tried power yoga, but you can't seem
to run in the lotus position.

....

Just when you finally got a few muscles,
the anorexic look comes back.

....

You pull a muscle getting on the stationary bicycle.

....

You're the only one in the room
wearing last year's leotard.

....

That cute guy on the treadmill turns out to be a girl.

....

The highest you can go on the StairMaster is "Wimp."

....

Your breast implants sag in the sauna.

....

You start your period while in the whirlpool.

....

During aerobics, the instructor says, "And for those of you who are out of shape, remember to take it easy," while looking right at you.

....

You know it's going to be a stressful divorce when:

He wants your frequent flyer miles.

....

You end up getting custody of his parents.

....

Yours is an "All Fault" divorce.

....

Your ex comes by to borrow money and you're
in a mud mask and those sweats that make
you look like Dom DeLuise.

....

He wants your Barbie collection.

....

Even that old standby, shopping, can be stressful. How about when:

You buy a body slimmer and you look fabulous
on the way to the emergency room.

....

You try on swimsuits, and you get
so frustrated you attempt to
slit your wrists with the price tag.

....

You buy a WonderBra and think it feels just like a mammogram.

....

You can't figure out how to attach your Depends to your thong underwear.

....

The talking scanner at the grocery store says, "Your total is $47.15, and that shirt doesn't go with that blouse."

....

The shoe salesman laughs when you say
you wear a size 7.

....

The clerk not only cuts your credit card in half,
she announces it over the loudspeaker.

....

You've just gotten into that tight Spandex
miniskirt in the dressing room and now
you have to go to the bathroom.

....

Your husband has come with you.

....

You're in the hardware store,
and except for the Studfinder,
there's nothing worth even looking at.

....

Oh, how lucky can you be? Stressed and PMS:

You think PMS stands for
....

• Probably a Mistake to wear Spandex

• Pack My Sword

• Potential Murder Suspect
....

You scoop double-fudge chocolate-chip ice cream
out of the carton with Doritos.

....

You get the cat fixed — again.

....

You cry all the way through
"America's Funniest Home Videos."

....

You're so bloated, your husband
built you a retaining wall.

....

Your inner child has cramps.

....

Your idea of primal screaming is
calling up your mother and yelling,
"This is all your fault."

....

The only salty things in the house
are the dog biscuits — you know,
you tried some last month.

....

Stress and dieting

We women are always either dieting or thinking about dieting or being told we should diet or recovering from a diet. It's enough to make you scream. Especially if:

....

You've found the forty pounds Oprah lost.

....

Your idea of a balanced meal is
a SlimFast and a Diet Coke.

....

Your husband shows you a picture of a twelve-year old model and says, "You know, you could look like this if you really wanted to." So you show him a picture of John Wayne Bobbit and say, "You know, you could look like this, if I really wanted you to."

....

You would have bowled a perfect game
if your fingers hadn't gotten stuck
in your bowling ball.

....

You just found out that fat-free cheesecake you've been scarfing down all year isn't.

....

You've been telling everyone that the reason you're putting on weight is to beef up for a movie role.

....

Stress and bad hair:

Your stylist keeps a list of her clients'
blood types taped to the mirror.

....

You get sued by your salon for damaging
their reputation.

....

You use more Drano than shampoo.

....

They've discontinued your haircolor —
"Natural Blonde, No Really, No. 17."

....

Your new hairstyle makes you look like
Susan Powter on a bad hair day.

....

Your favorite place to have your face, hair, and nails
done is called "Hostile Makeovers."

....

Stress and health care:

Your New-Age dentist asks you to visualize
your gums getting numb.

········

The X-ray machine catches fire
during your mammogram.

········

The last time you went to a doctor, a CAT scan was
what you did at night before you went to bed.

········

Your dentist has a sign in the lobby that says
No PAIN, NO GAIN.

. . . .

Your new gynecologist turns out to be the guy you
broke off the engagement with.

. . . .

The speculum has icicles.

. . . .

*. . . Ok, your break is over. Now go back to your job,
your laundry, your root canal, your tax audit, your aerobics class
. . . or whatever we interrupted!*